My Son, My Savior

My Son, My Savior

The Awesome Wonder of Jesus' Birth

CALVIN MILLER
Illustrated by Ron DiCianni

Chariot VICTOR
PUBLISHING
A DIVISION OF COOK COMMUNICATIONS

To my friend, Randy Maid,
who asked me to do these paintings ten years ago.
He didn't realize that
God was using him to point me
in the direction I was supposed to go.
I will be forever grateful for his obedience and foresight.
To God be the glory!

R.D.

Chariot Books is an imprint of ChariotVictor Publishing,
A division of Cook Communications, Colorado Springs, Colorado 80918
Cook Communications, Paris, Ontario
Kingsway Communications, Eastbourne, England

MY SON, MY SAVIOR
© 1997 by Calvin Miller for text and David C. Cook Publishing Company for illustrations.

Designed by Andrea Boven
Illustrations by Ron DiCianni

The art was originally created in 1988 by Ron DiCianni for Bible-in-Life Sunday School curriculum.

This story is taken from Matthew 1:18—2:23 and Luke 1:26—2:40.

Scripture verses used on pages 5 and 32 are taken from the *Holy Bible: New International Version®*.
Copyright 1973, 1978, 1984 by International Bible Society.
Used by permission of Zondervan Publishing House. All rights reserved.

First printing, 1997
Printed in Hong Kong
01 00 99 98 97   5 4 3 2 1

Published in association with the literary agency of Alive Communications, Inc.,
1465 Kelly Johnson Blvd., Suite 320, Colorado Springs, CO 80920

"For to us
a child is born,
to us
a son is given."

ISAIAH 9:6

I have a son at last.
His name is Jesus.
He is a special baby
given to the world
but passing into it
through the circle of my arms.
Sometimes when I look at him,
he seems so little, so defenseless.

When I wonder at the mystery of such a little soul,
I am overwhelmed.
I stand in awe before this infant majesty.
Who could ever fathom this wonder—
why God, the Almighty One,
would reduce Himself to utter helplessness.
I thrill to think
that He who is the very image of God Himself
cannot even move unless I carry him.

I often gaze upon him while he sleeps.
I look and shudder each time I realize
that he is God's Son,
the long-awaited Messiah with a local dusty address,
living here in Bethlehem
with me and Joseph.
He seems so ordinary,
so very much like other babies I have known
that I often must stop to remember
that he is so much more than others can imagine him to be.

Here there is a mystery of splendor—
That I have had a baby, and yet am chaste.
"Mother." I knew the word ahead of time,
before I knew the word "wife."
Such was the miracle:
God folded Himself into a tiny form
and here, within myself, the vast Creator defined Himself
in the simple three-letter word "boy."

I love God and have always desired to please Him.
But I see myself as no heroine of Israel.
Yet this great honor came to me:
God made of me a door
and made His entrance into time through my poor body.
Some doubt the miracle by asking *how?*
How is a fool's question if God is truly God.
How is really a kind of blasphemy
by which weak mortals demand that God explain Himself
to the unbelieving.

My question was not *how* but *why?*
No, it was really *why me?*
Grace is the only answer.
Grace is a stubborn, lovely flower
that picks the harshest deserts in which to bloom.
So heaven came to me,
bringing gifts too real to doubt,
too wonderful to be explained.
God—flesh-wrapped
in splendor—who like the midday sun
is too intense to stare at

lest the overwhelming brilliance
blind the eye.

In the fourteenth year of the Emperor Augustus—
near twilight on an insignificant day,
of that insignificant year—
I was alone in the dark,
in the confining sitting room
of our house in Nazareth.
I was just sitting there,
meditating on the Messiah.
Like nearly all of the Jews I know,
I was rather eager that He come.

Oh how we Jews needed God to show up!
We were downcast.
We doubted the hope we needed to live.
We told ourselves so often
in our little synagogues
that God had forgotten His people.
It is hard to believe that you are loved of God
when you are hated by those
who hold political sway.
Sometimes we doubted that God would come in time
to save Israel before the Romans destroyed it.

The Romans!
How tired we were of their swaggering arrogance.

Meditating upon the suffering of Israel,
I breathed half-aloud,

"Lord, this would be a good time
for You to send Your Messiah.
When will You save Your people?"

"Greetings," said a voice behind me.
I spun around in the half-light of the darkening room.
There stood a man I had never seen.
An aura of light swept the ceiling above his head.
My breath stopped!
"Greetings, you who are highly favored!
The Lord is with you!"

I was terrified!
I begged my mind to tell me
who this being really was.
Why had he come to my house?
What had he meant by that odd phrase,
"You who are highly favored"?

I felt much too small
to respond to such an imposing visitor.
My words were nearly paralyzed
as my body trembled.
The awesomeness of the moment
was almost more than I could bear.

"Don't be afraid!" said the angel.

Gabriel went on,
"Mary, you have found favor with God.
You will have a child and give birth to a son,

and you are to give him the name Jesus.
He will be great and will be called
the Son of the Most High.
The Lord God will give Him the throne of His father David,
and He will reign over the house of Jacob forever.
His kingdom will never end."

At last I spoke as one coming out of a stupor,
"How can this happen, since I am a virgin?"

I learned that evening that if God could explain
Himself to human beings, He would be less
of a God than human beings need.
"The Holy Spirit will come upon you," he said,
"and the power of the Most High will overshadow you.
So the Holy One to be born from you
will be called the Son of God."

Gabriel paused.
He knew I needed time
to sort through this sheaf of mysteries
and set his words in order.

"Even Elizabeth, your relative,
is going to have a child
in her old age, and she,
who is said to be barren,
is already in her sixth month.
For nothing is impossible with God."

All I could say was,
"May it be to me as you have said."

When I looked up, my visitor was gone.
It was awhile before my mind
stopped churning with Gabriel's confrontation.
But when it did, I thought immediately of Joseph.
Joseph, my friend! My fiancé!

"Joseph!" I shuddered
as his face rose like a ghost
in the smoky mirror of my mind.
"How will you ever understand?"

I told Joseph.
He did not understand.
Worse, he did not believe me.
"Angels, Mary?
Please, no angels!
Angels are the stuff of dreams—
they never show up in Nazareth
except in rabbis' sermons."

Joseph, my needy carpenter, was a practical man
who drove solid pegs into solid boards.
He saw my pregnancy as evidence
that I had been unfaithful.
His struggling heart became
the battlefield of love and logic.

I have never seen a man so broken.

His brokenness contributed to my pain.
I was torn of soul when he told me
he would have to break our engagement.

It was at this time
that my good and kind Joseph
was to have a visit of his own.
One of those angels
he had taken such a stand against
left the rabbis' sermons
and came to him saying,
"Joseph, you son of David,
don't be afraid to take Mary as your wife
for she shall have a son
and you shall call His name Jesus
for He shall save His people
from their sins!"

Joseph returned to me a broken man.
He gave me back his promise of unending love—
a humble feast served upon the table of his soul.
If contrition is the bread of lovers,
we devoured the loaf.

In the ensuing months,
there came an empire-wide enrollment.
It was tax time throughout Augustus' world.

We were required by Augustus' law
to make a pilgrimage
to Joseph's ancestral home of Bethlehem.
The Romans would not allow for any excuses—
all must make some journey.
All must be enrolled—all.
No matter that I was in the last weeks of my pregnancy.
The arduous journey must be made.
I was glad that God had given to me
this carpenter named Joseph.
Joseph seemed strong and robust,
with hands that swung a hammer or an ax,
and yet could gently reach to touch my shoulders.

It pains me to admit that I complained.
"I cannot make this trip.
Our baby is too near."

"Mary, I'll be with you,
and God goes just ahead of us.
He will be faithful, even as the prophet said;
He will bear you up on eagle's wings.
Do you suppose He would ask you
to be mother to the Son of God
and not protect and guard that Son?"

And so we went.
My carpenter, philosopher—
my carpenter, protector—and myself.
I knew that Joseph was right.
We had a date with God in Bethlehem.
In fact, all the world had a date with God in Bethlehem,
and the date could not be postponed.
Augustus himself played his role in this event
and never knew he served the living God.

The Judean roads were crowded;
the inns were always full.
As we drew near to Bethlehem,
I began to feel the pain of childbirth
settling down upon me.
Joseph could tell I was uncomfortable
and knew our son would soon be born.
We hurried into that unfriendly place.
He knocked on every door in the city
in the attempt to find us a room.
But alas, the city was so thronged
by others who must pay their taxes,
there were no rooms available.
Only one innkeeper, learning of my condition,
offered us any help at all,
and the most that he could do
was to volunteer his stable-cave.

It seemed ungracious and yet
how grateful we were for this little space
out of the cold night air.

We had not been there for long when Jesus came.
At last, the pain stopped,
and then generously,
like the first warm rain of spring,
joy came.

Engulfed in that joy, we were oblivious to all else.
We could not know that outside of town
the skies split open with angels.
They announced to a group of shepherds
with terrifying volume
that the three of us were in the stable-cave.
The Savior had been born.

They came,
these rustic men, staring at the baby I held.
Their gaze became transfixed.
Then they seemed to be under an odd compulsion
to obey some distant mandate which they barely understood.
Not knowing exactly what to do, they fidgeted awkwardly.
Then they began falling to their knees,
casting their eyes momentarily away from Jesus
as though what they saw was too holy to look upon.
Tears fell unashamed across their sunbaked faces
as though the child were theirs.
This was a look I would get used to in time.
Was the baby mine or not?

I thought so.
And yet,
if you could have seen their faces,
you would have thought the child was theirs.
These rustic field hands
were the first to teach me
that this boy I held belonged to all.

The shepherds' adoration
had an oddly quieting effect on me.
I could see that in their own uncomplicated way
these simple men understood
the importance of this night.
They said their celebration was the subject
of whole skies of angels
singing their grand hallelujahs.
"Ma'am," said one of the shepherds,
"we don't see angels much,
and I found myself asking
on the way into town
why angels would appear to
a grimy bunch of herders like ourselves."

"It's grace," I told them, "all of grace!
God comes to all of us
with gifts too immense for us to understand."

I laughed when one of the men told me
that the angels loudly ordered them not to be afraid.
"It was a little late to tell us that!" the shepherd grinned.

I looked down at my new baby boy.
We all did.
Jesus was sleeping soundly.

A second time the shepherds gazed upon my child
and once again bowed down.
Then they shuffled out,
quietly into the night.

It takes awhile for new *parents*
to learn to wear the word.
But at those rare moments
when I could leave off thinking
about Jesus being the Son of God,
I enjoyed thinking
about his being the son of me and Joseph.
We were, after all, a real family.
One mother, one father, one child.
Families do not use grand words
to speak to each other.
I was discovering that being a mommy
holds a special warmth
that in some ways transcended
the notion of being some kind of holy vessel.
And Joseph was simply—yet wonderfully—daddy.
He felt the way I did.
Even in the first few days after Jesus was born
I could see him thinking to himself,
as all daddies must,
"I'm going to make a carpenter out of Jesus,
whom we shall call our little Joshua."

One night he was rocking Jesus
right after his midnight feeding,
and I overheard him say,
"Go to sleep, my little Josh,
you gotta get your rest
if you're gonna learn to use a hammer and a saw."

The statement seemed most natural to him.
He had every daddy's dream of wanting his son
to be like himself.
But what I found most difficult
was trying to fit together the fact
that the angel had called him
the Son of the Most High
while Joseph called him Josh.
Infant messiahs may be princes in heaven,
but they remain simply babies
in the wonderful togetherness
that is a family.

Jesus seemed so honestly "Josh"
that I had to force myself to remember what Gabriel said:
"He will be great and will be called
the Son of the Most High.
The Lord God will give Him the throne of His father David,
and He will reign over the house of Jacob forever.
His kingdom will never end."
So Joseph and I never saw ourselves as a "holy family."
That was the stuff angels sang about on hillsides.
No, we were just a family, Joseph and I and Josh.

It has to be that way, 'cause you can't go around
thinking of yourself in high and mighty ways.
There's midnight feedings sometimes, and diapers all the time.
And then there's the question of politics and taxes,
which is why we were in Bethlehem in the first place.
If our little family had historical significance,
God would have to point that out in His way and in His time.

In the meantime,
Jesus would learn
to walk, to talk, and later have his *bar mitzvah*.
And Joseph, true to all his dreams,
would teach Jesus to use the hammer.
I would try to keep him in warm, dry clothes
so that he could stay fit and well
for those grand purposes
that heaven had in mind for him.

Life was wide in all its dimensions,
and after Joseph managed to pay his enrollment tax,
we decided we'd stay where we were for awhile.
Then Joseph made up his mind to begin practicing
his trade in Bethlehem.
The town was near the city of Jerusalem
so it appeared he would have plenty of work.

Once the enrollment was over, we left the cave
as housing became more available.
I was glad when we found another home,
for life seemed to return to normal
once Joseph began working again.

On the eighth day of Jesus' life
we went to present him at the temple.
An odd and beautiful thing happened.
There was an old man named Simeon
who had lived for most of the century.
He was well known in the city,
especially by all of those
who frequented the temple.
It was generally believed
that God was keeping the old man alive
until such time as the Messiah would come to Israel.
He was, by all popular consent,
the one who would identify the Messiah when He came.
Most people thought he would point out
some robust and winsome young zealot
who could levy large Jewish armies
and teach Rome a thing or two about Jewish heritage.
But Simeon was so schooled
in the ways of God
that he was able to spot God's Son,
even when He came wrapped in swaddling clothes,
as easily as he could have
if the Messiah had come astride a steed.

I will never forget
this wonderful eighth day of Jesus' life.
I was leaning on Joseph,
still a little weak from having given birth.
And as we walked up to the temple,
this fearsome old man
approached us like a thundering prophet.

When he reached out to take our baby,
I was paralyzed by fear.
I certainly didn't want any stranger
to touch our little Jesus.
I drew away from Simeon, furiously protective.
But somehow my motherly instincts
were put to rest.
I still can't believe what I did next.
I willingly extended my little, bundled boy to the old man.
Light washed down across his leathery old face.
He stopped and held the baby.
His tears fell like liquid light
on the boy's blankets.
He stared and smiled and wept
as a large crowd began to gather around the four of us.
Then his smile broadened even further.
He held up Jesus toward the heavens,
as though the entire sky was God's blue altar.
"Behold!" he cried.
His opaque eyelids were glazed with brightness as he shouted
half to the heavens and half to those gathered about us.
"Now let me depart in peace
for my eyes have seen the salvation of God!"

Suddenly all things were wrapped in joy.
The Messiah was on earth!
Simeon had confirmed it.

Simeon reminded me
that Joseph and I could never be merely a family.

We were somehow actors in a pageant
so big that only God could have written it.
We were like performers in a Roman drama,
acting out cosmic truths
in a dingy little theater of human hope.

A strange and wonderful old man
was holding my baby.
And Simeon, like the shepherds, reminded me again
that Jesus wasn't only my baby.
He belonged to a family bigger than mine.
And Simeon was telling a truth bigger than my truth.

Simeon handed Jesus back to me
and turned and walked away.

Other things lay ahead.
In time, kings from the east would come,
offering us the treasure that
would make our brief exile in Egypt possible.
Herod would send his soldiers to massacre the children.
The future was all joy and apprehension
mingled in a single chalice of saving love.

But for now I had a baby.
Even as his little hands reached
to clutch my hair and pat my face,
I knew that God's only beloved
was in my arms as surely as
God Himself was in the world.

Tell me this, are *God* and *grace* spelled differently?
I think not.
Are not both of them our mentors
to teach us who we are?
It is grace alone that helped me find my place
in the unsearchable purposes of God.
Over the next three decades,
I would awake for ten thousand mornings
to bless God that He had chosen to use
such a simple thing as motherhood
to bring all people to Himself.
And when my son was grown,
he would teach the world
that his Father was a God of gentle love,
not by strutting in the crowded arenas
of human self-importance,
but reaching with his strong young hands
to do a mighty thing.
Till then God Himself would wrap
all of human joy in baby laughter.
And after this joy
in centuries to come,
many nations will bow
before the awesome wonder
of a mother and her child. ❧

*"She will give birth to a son,
and you are to give him the name Jesus,
because he will save his people from their sins."*

MATTHEW 1:21

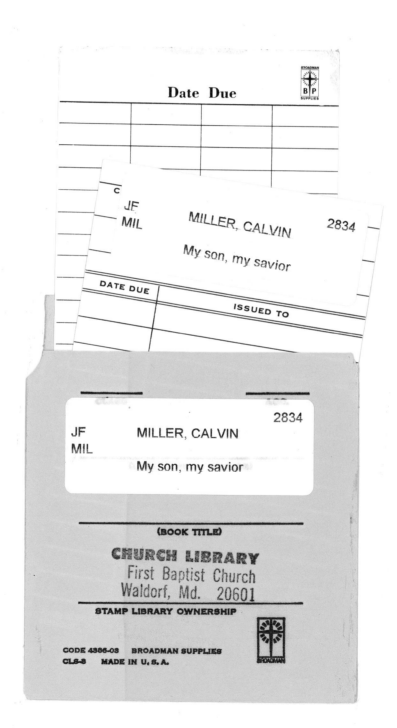

Date Due

BROADMAN
B P
SUPPLIES

C

JF
MIL

MILLER, CALVIN

2834

My son, my savior

DATE DUE

ISSUED TO

2834

JF
MIL

MILLER, CALVIN

My son, my savior

(BOOK TITLE)